Monet's Bamboo

Mike Jurkovic

Monet's Bamboo

Mike Jurkovic

Copyright © 2024 by Mike Jurkovic. All rights reserved. No part of this publication may be reproduced, distributed, or transmitted in any form or by any means, including photocopying, recording, or other electronic or mechanical methods, without the prior written permission of the publisher, except in the case of brief quotations embodied in critical reviews and certain other non-commercial uses permitted by copyright law. For permission requests, write to the publishers, addressed "Attention: Permissions" at mjpj55@gmail.com

This is a work of creative nonfiction. Many details, including all personal identifying information, have been changed to protect the privacy of the individuals involved.

Ordering Information:
 For details, contact monetsbamboo@gmail.com

Print ISBN: 978-0-9973258-8-1

Printed in the United States of America
 First Edition

Photographs: Mike Jurkovic

Book design and production: smallpackages.com

Monet's bamboo

*I don't consider traditional form. No artist totally ever has,
nor should, lock themselves in that way. I love to edit, so
I keep the three line, 5-7-5, seventeen syllable perspective
fixed on the horizon and prune longer pieces to the core
of what I hoped to say or, better yet, the moment demanded,
or, as Garcia sings Hunter "Once in a while / You get
shown the light / In the strangest of places /
If you look at it right."*

mj '24

Beginning

Before reading Monet's Bamboo, my experience of Mike Jurkovic's poems was akin to strapping in for a parachute jump. As soon as he steps up to a microphone, I feel wind in my hair and a clap of nylon bursting open from behind. But I know I'm safe. Mike's acumen for tough realities is tempered with a compassion that's only transmissible from the heart of a qualified survivor.

> I hear my father's
> voice as I near the age he
> took leave   without qualm

I was intrigued when Mike began sharing his haiku publicly. His grittiest work has always been infused with a haggard tenderness. That tone is ably reframed into these gently polished poems, where the original stone is palpable beneath the poet's burnishing hand. This piece embodies Mike's ease with fusing moxie and humility, underpinned by a gutsy enjambment:

> I cannot hinder
> God no matter the shit I
> stir   how hard I try

The persona behind such an insight has no truck with sacred-vs.-profane; all the stuff of life is game for poetic alchemy. Reaching for the stars in his private backyard of the mind, Mike keeps feet to the sod where we all live, search, fail, make do, and sometimes triumph over our worst resistance to be human.

> steep is steeper than
> years ago but my old heart
> keeps climbing up hill

These haiku capture the essence of wabi-sabi, the Japanese principle of temporal beauty: nothing lasts, nothing's ever finished, nothing and no one is perfect. Mike's wabi-sabi is a poetic habit tuned to the transience of youth, plans, and consciousness itself—the skill of extracting nectar from loss.

Monet's Bamboo is proof the modern sage walks alongside us, whistling his poems into the wind. Syllable by syllable, these haiku arouse in us a need to pay closest regard to the least likely object of attention. And recognize ourselves in a leaf, a riverbed stone, an unanswered question, a rusted Chevy in a cornfield.

As Sam Beckett summed it up, the artist's job comes down to "Ever tried. Ever failed. No matter. Try again. Fail again. Fail better." As Mike Jurkovic demonstrates, there is no "fail" in haiku—there is but the thankful labor of attention.

> I need only work
> with one basket empty it
> fill it empty it

Stephanie JT Russell
   author, *One Flash of Lightning /*
   a samurai path for living the moment

Mike Jurkovic

Monet's Bamboo

hear Monet's bamboo
pray the wind the birdsong of
Giverny ascends

Mike Jurkovic

between judgement and
mercy a state of grace the
compassionate one

Monet's Bamboo

the world does its work
sways the hay grass shakes the trees
holds the leaves alight

Mike Jurkovic

        and here he painted
        floating lilies languishing
        still quiet water

a park in Paris
new sun bridal wreathe cherry
lilacs all in bloom

Mike Jurkovic

hear the quiet tide
the ages of years laid bare the
call of life renewed

Monet's Bamboo

only I bring sin
to fruition betray trust
faith   my one true self

Mike Jurkovic

the less memory
I hold onto all the more
discoveries found

to the wonder of
who I am I bare my heart
to the morning sun

Mike Jurkovic

french girls laughing make
the world stop and smile tired hearts
sing old men rejoice

Monet's Bamboo

I cannot describe
this moment finally free
of definition

Mike Jurkovic

eventually
the pebble on riverbed
causes me no pain

Monet's Bamboo

where the quiet soul
goes is here God's place of peace
birds bullfrogs chipmunks

Mike Jurkovic

       the faces in the trees
       the faces in the stone whole
       forest comes to life

Monet's Bamboo

day wakes work begins
forgiving yesterday is
a thing of the past

Mike Jurkovic

every labor a
learning   every learning a
few steps closer home

highland fog descends
dense grey green clouds of morning
blanket milton road

Mike Jurkovic

with my child's eye no
gluttony betrays me no
hatred consumes me

Monet's Bamboo

seasons take their toll
here   fell the forest   bare the
bedrock   forgive all

Mike Jurkovic

gather the moments
my friends they are all that is
bidden us partake

Monet's Bamboo

Monet's bamboo sweeps
the twilight sky   its brushwork
paints the maiden moon

Mike Jurkovic

    the oak tree's simple
    majesty captures sunrise
    frees its fleeting soul

Monet's Bamboo

like the blue of your
eyes before you passed silent
deep fearless forward

Mike Jurkovic

        branch grabs sky holds grey
        cloud against new blue against
        the brightening sky

Monet's Bamboo

I see your colors
the late apples hold the young
chill   sumac and pine

Mike Jurkovic

there are faint moments
few and far between when you
see the open path

Monet's Bamboo

we are each others
work each others passion our
harbors at days end

Mike Jurkovic

    these are the days you
    find yourself grateful they are
    in this world with you

Monet's Bamboo

the chatter of leaves
undoes my thoughts   leaves me clear
to start once again

Mike Jurkovic

we are pilgrims works
in progress simple servants
of this bright new day

Monet's Bamboo

haunts and whispers taunts
quivers sketches of rain such
is the length of days

Mike Jurkovic

       let me be found where
       I fall   in new footsteps   no
       old dreams in pocket

I am because of
others their love their ashes
this breeze on this hill

Mike Jurkovic

again spring's early
seekers crocus peepers the
turmoil of all souls

Monet's Bamboo

prayers weave through these
woods rising   rising prayers
to Heaven   weaving

Mike Jurkovic

touched by forgiveness
spine shimmers   love arises
my thoughts clear again

Monet's Bamboo

water lilies and
turtles in the rain the whole
world moves without me

Mike Jurkovic

blue hydrangeas sea
side roses   sunrise seagulls
ocean moon fading

Monet's Bamboo

like winter took
the tallest trees   I will not grieve
should I fall right here

Mike Jurkovic

Monet's bamboo   cool
breeze gardens flower blue
yellow purple gold

Monet's Bamboo

a warm grace buoys
the ajo leaves descent like
mine graceful to ground

Mike Jurkovic

like God's own garden
wrens feed in ours grackles crow
bluebirds fill the sky

Monet's Bamboo

it glows like Heaven
doesn't it Dad harvest sun
upon Crystal Lake

Mike Jurkovic

still leaves before wind
gusts swirl storm whirls at my feet
the dance continues

a pesky summer
Hudson Valley breeze blows your
skirt above your knees

Mike Jurkovic

a soft cadence fills
the room and it is you there
at my side still strong

Monet's Bamboo

they said the clouds   would
move in and here they come now
westward   shadow slide

Mike Jurkovic

        no such thing as a
        New York girl   they all spring from
        Buddha's great wide heart

Monet's Bamboo

like an old couple
two clouds kiss merge become whole
fill the sky with love

Mike Jurkovic

with all windows closed
the honeysuckle sneaks through
into our kitchen

Monet's Bamboo

having scaled the sharp
cliffs of gravity   I pee
over the far side

Mike Jurkovic

       top o' the mornin
       little cat   did God whisper
       into your ear too

Monet's Bamboo

here was my first hint
of freedom sky above lake
quiet calling blue

Mike Jurkovic

       like me   this tree was
       always here   like me this tree
       returns to the earth

Monet's Bamboo

empty your pockets
empty your mind fill your heart
with today's promise

Mike Jurkovic

as candles undo
dusk   the brine of rhetoric
undoes all reason

Monet's Bamboo

we are a tangle
of blankets legs arms mind hearts
all our private parts

Mike Jurkovic

ocean chews stone and
time to sand   will I ever
know such momentum

Monet's Bamboo

Monet's bamboo keeps
the shade dapples the lupine
iris and tulip

Mike Jurkovic

the sound of winter
free of seething free of siege
long days receding

Monet's Bamboo

tis fall   the peace flags
shed their color like leaves they
hold tight against wind

Mike Jurkovic

river roses neath
brooklyn bridge summer girls smile
world is right again

Monet's Bamboo

big wind blows and blows
and keeps the clouds tumbling round
and round big blue sky

Mike Jurkovic

already autumn
wilted green   spotted yellow
the woodbine crimson

a menage a trois
of beetles   banging beneath
a clutch of oak leaves

Mike Jurkovic

wild keening rock 'n
roll our names enameled on
East 14th West 3rd

Monet's Bamboo

my secrets need not
define me carry over
a pattern of years

Mike Jurkovic

the upward calling
points me east   birdsong summon
the new morning prayer

Monet's Bamboo

woodpecker in the
nearness   eastern sky waking
I stand in its midst

Mike Jurkovic

since you asked   here is
my mantra   no one's helpless
when they stop to pray

Monet's Bamboo

from here I can see
myself flying   the angel
I will someday be

Mike Jurkovic

days end evensong
psalms   quiet prayer   and her
body next to mine

Monet's bamboo shades
his perennials scatters
light the dahlias

Mike Jurkovic

night comes to the dark
Catskills   Dylan skids   big bear
shadows out the moon

ghostly Taos moon
doesn't know it's morning yet
hangs in sunshine sky

Mike Jurkovic

ancestral home   the
buffalo thorn spirit and
wisdom grace this land

Monet's Bamboo

cold river and sky
grey looming unforgiving
the train in between

Mike Jurkovic

        some poets fixate
        on grateful sunset others
        the raw stormy dawn

autumn's blue rain mists
Gertude's Nose   rolls erratic
into the valley

Mike Jurkovic

cute in that lazy
way women have of holding
sway   so long after

Monet's Bamboo

ice forest sparkles
in new sun what more have I
slept through wept through dreamt

Mike Jurkovic

she asleep as I
tell this tale a story true
a fine love complete

Monet's Bamboo

the stubborn moon pales
towards redemption   I sit
hoping for the day

Mike Jurkovic

        it's a poet's way
        to wander   wonder the mountains
        in search for new light

Monet's Bamboo

we pass these dry hours
no rain in sight   no deluge
sweeps our heat away

Mike Jurkovic

how long can we fight
god's war   before surrendering
to his gracious peace

Monet's Bamboo

through stained glass mornings
we wander so unaware
of mercy shining

Mike Jurkovic

you are God's gift to
yourself before becoming
your gift back to God

Monet's Bamboo

I hear my father's
voice as I near the age he
took leave   without qualm

Mike Jurkovic

remain faithful not
fearful   the darkness shall pass
joy will shine again

Monet's Bamboo

I need only work
with one basket empty it
fill it empty it

Mike Jurkovic

I can smell the wet
earth of the dark valley the
old sun to the west

Monet's Bamboo

the movement of souls
through summer leaves the soft air
ripples curls shimmers

Mike Jurkovic

        worry worry   all
        for naught   for each day its own
        trouble   its own grace

Brahms Symphony 4
chaperones the breeze borne leaves
watch the angels dance

Mike Jurkovic

    the storm between two
    stirs riles roils quiets subsides
    the storm between two

Monet's Bamboo

my antics of no
import on the general
motion of the world

Mike Jurkovic

what kindling then   shall
we set alight   as the moon
above   darks the night

Monet's Bamboo

it takes some years to
find the words   so let us talk
now about our love

Mike Jurkovic

when will we make room
at the common well for all
to wash   replenish

Monet's Bamboo

the unforgiving
work of revolution is
in all of our hands

Mike Jurkovic

my girl our house three
cool cats make a fine end to
a long hard won day

Monet's Bamboo

among leaves I sit
as I will someday lie in
the welcoming earth

Mike Jurkovic

so much more beyond
this cloud of mind noise of war
of men dividing

Monet's Bamboo

I slip lysergic
facing west fond of flashback
and first awe sunset

Mike Jurkovic

when sunflowers fall
it breaks her heart young girl sad
when sunflowers fall

Monet's Bamboo

facing west in these
green pastures   an instrument
of peace   forever

Mike Jurkovic

sometimes consciousness
is a heavy messy thing
better times   weightless

Monet's Bamboo

I cannot hinder
God no matter the shit I
stir   how hard I try

Mike Jurkovic

we crisscross we do
on this flight path of angels
dance careen caress

Monet's Bamboo

it was your hands in
mine this morning holding this
old frayed book of prayer

Mike Jurkovic

rouse each other to
good work now that the darkness
draws ever more near

Monet's Bamboo

steep is steeper than
years ago but my old heart
keeps climbing up hill

Mike Jurkovic

I stand in witness
to sky   cliff   immovable
stone Heaven's grand scale

Monet's Bamboo

a lonely muscle
our hearts a lively muscle
our hearts strong our hearts

Mike Jurkovic

against the city
we shout the words that turn
the world   shake the sky

Monet's Bamboo

if you heard this one
stop me I repeat myself
as these days shorten

Mike Jurkovic

coveted two hawks
their voyage   cloud bank bumpers
bend their flight   hold true

Monet's Bamboo

the commotion of
America goes on and
on   unceasingly

Mike Jurkovic

the weight of conscience
burdens no politician
only who they serve

Monet's Bamboo

the eastern pavements
decant the morning sun ring
with our common songs

Mike Jurkovic

hear the mourning doves
not my trilling   my cackle
inadequate plea

Monet's Bamboo

beneath a slate grey
sky fire fell upon me the
new forgiving day

Mike Jurkovic

how did I draw the
short straw and win this life this
this love   full   with you

an artisan bowl
of pasta and parmesan
is still mac and cheese

Mike Jurkovic

the acorn rain falls
new this morning winter comes
fast the squirrels know

Monet's Bamboo

after another
snake bit season   the pile up
of years   blocks the sun

Mike Jurkovic

cooing stars my poems
ascend towards yon pale moon
celestial song

Monet's Bamboo

each body its own
time   its own mind   its thoughts   its doubts
its heart   its own love

Mike Jurkovic

autumn in august
the owl hunts sings a dark blues
echoes the slow moon

Monet's Bamboo

footprints old behind
us   footprints new   ahead   we
never walk alone

Mike Jurkovic

late august light finds
a gypsy violin its
music so restless

periwinkle morn
moon fades fog lifts pigeon choir
weeds   thorns apples ripe

Mike Jurkovic

God cannot lead us
all into battle   but each
will claim his banner

woodbine   ivy   turn
first   the moon's complexion wanes
east wind   cornstalk   pine

Mike Jurkovic

if nothing matters
dharma son why so many
ways to make coffee

Monet's Bamboo

the fuchsia will not
tell the hummingbird's secrets
honeysuckle mute

Mike Jurkovic

melodies of light
the joy of your face the sky
reflecting heaven

Monet's Bamboo

the earth yields without
fanfare   so must I too learn
to harvest in kind

Mike Jurkovic

bell chimes on dad's clock
in synchronization with
the change of season

Kerouac and the
road ahead   freeway scramble
4th gear   manifold

Mike Jurkovic

traces of lipstick
on the moon   a quiet snow
my small wish for you

Monet's Bamboo

the bard owl howls and
everything in the forest
turns its head to hear

Mike Jurkovic

red ulster apples
early browning leaves cool breeze
dancing uncut hay

bellow the morning
bewilder   befuddle God's
least expectations

Mike Jurkovic

cumulus cruise the
Mohonk sky the flight path of
angels passes through

Monet's Bamboo

a steadying rain
soaked my books wildflowers in
the gray sky tremble

Mike Jurkovic

deliriously
romantic   this valley morn
as Luna awakes

Monet's Bamboo

o gone spirits were
you skinny dipping   rising
mists from big sky lake

Mike Jurkovic

heron rising through
late winter fog   another
lost soul confessing

Monet's Bamboo

smile at the glitches
soon the moon the stars the sun
will join your laughter

Mike Jurkovic

take nothing as you
travel   poet earns his keep
warrior walks light

Monet's Bamboo

crescent moon illumines
this hill where we love feed the
cats watch lilies grow

Mike Jurkovic

      live these last days free
      of enmity   indictment
      tirade invective

Monet's Bamboo

Monet's bamboo sings
song   through tall grass zephyr
sweeps   his cherries tart

Mike Jurkovic

       it is not just a
       life you live it is a song
       to be sung by all

Monet's Bamboo

one more body part
flies the coop breaks down needs
new meds begs repair

Mike Jurkovic

    she arrived like all
    girls with dark brown hair and sea
    green eyes arrive   late

Monet's Bamboo

there should be wonder
in your every step if not
retrace your pathway

Mike Jurkovic

the holy hudson
valley where bomb trains rattle
humble western shore

Monet's Bamboo

the forest is breaking
each day a new tree cracks the
old guard falls away

Mike Jurkovic

a spirit passes
overhead leaves flutter some
fall into silence

Monet's Bamboo

your back porch prayers
answered   mine too given a
warm and kind reply

Mike Jurkovic

a heartened prayer a
poppy tune a pretty girl
smiles and jogs on by

Monet's Bamboo

wing to wing combat
crows v. hawk swoop swirl swipe bang
boom zoom caw caw caw

Mike Jurkovic

    soft and breathing she
    gives me perspective she dreams
    news stars in the sky

Monet's Bamboo

Mike Jurkovic

Monet's Bamboo

Mike Jurkovic

www.ingramcontent.com/pod-product-compliance
Lightning Source LLC
Chambersburg PA
CBHW030437010526
44118CB00011B/672